D1563442

Roundabout Directions to Lincoln Center

Renée K. Nicholson

Crossroads Poetry Series
Detroit, Michigan, USA
Windsor, Ontario, Canada

Published in the United States of America and Canada by

Urban Farmhouse Press.
www.urbanfarmhousepress.com

First Edition

ISBN: 978-0-9937690-0-9

Book cover design: D.A. Lockhart
Layout: D.A. Lockhart

The Crossroads Poetry Series is a line books that showcases established and emerging poetic voices from across North America. The books in this series represent what the editors at UFP believe to be some of the strongest voices in both American and Canadian poetics.

For Matt

Contents

Roundabout Directions to Lincoln Center

Danskin tights with seams
down the back, drying
in the window. New York's
flannel-pinstripe February hums
with traffic.

Call them care packages: doodles
and comics, snippets of song
lyrics: There is a light
and it never goes out. Bootleg
cassette tapes of punk-pop
from the Cameo, played
until they snap now hidden
in shoeboxes stuffed in the attic.

Gone too—grand jété,
my right knee, a boy
who flew airplanes
and crashed somewhere over
Colorado. My friend Lex—

who all the girls liked, hanged
when he turned 21.
Granddad's sour-dough
buckwheat cakes, tasted tart
as childhood: sweat and running and
afternoon storms. Remember a piggy
bank from Sharky's Pizza, stuffed
with hope and pennies. I thought

I could save for a bus ticket
and would go, no matter what
the cost. The metallic clank
of another deposit to those ears
chimes of devotion and worship.
Fifth floor walkup, walls too close
for my single bed ambition. Tights
over chair backs, strewn
across the uneven planks
of the floor.

What I Didn't Need To Know

The week after I left the island,
it was Shark Week on Discovery.

Sure, I'd chosen to forget; in salty
surf, murky waters, there were apex

predators, the same way sex
is impossible, scalloped-edged, sad. Obscured

from view, it was a dolphin's dorsal
that crested the waves. In my pink cowgirl

pajamas, face illuminated by the flicker
of a tiger shark snatching an albatross at the surface,

I ached for the serrated rows of teeth.

The Body Is Basic

You are twice my age which is the point of wanting me;
I'm starving myself on purpose and can barely pay rent.

Your weakness is really my body, you negotiate—
your hands spatulas pressed to rump, the curve
of hip spooned out,

me, a slipper chair whose bones are not quite
modern or classic; more like Carlo's wooden masterpiece,
a coat hanger:

timber smoothed, arched, fabric draped over & sexy
in ways akin to fondling.

Tomorrow I eat your orange with regret. Peeled rind,
separating each segment sprays
its acidic & sweet

juice. Tart. Like touching parts
of a woman who doesn't want

you. Inherited Mollino: Carlo's shoebox stuffed—
2,000 naughty Polaroid's, this pharaoh prepared
his tomb for the afterlife—

leaving the simple items, but re-designed for pleasure,
the bounty's a fetish, but we are both in trade.

Primary Level

That is not the most efficient way—
Smile. Only beautiful people can
dance.

Mrs. Ferragamo and Mrs. Gucci had hair
big, shellacked, like Designing Women,
& would not tilt their heads in port de bras.
Christmas in Italy, he swore, was extravagant—

oh, the gifts.

Turn-out makes it; only
your nose traces a rainbow.
Like the tomato
in tomato sauce, but not everyone
is meant to be a dancer.

Pas de chat is one way, gibberish
to the French.

Cecchetti and Vaganova fist fight
in purgatory. Lift your heart
to the angels—

Accept this unmaking.

Filigree

Today I wash our shot glasses, the green
with the gold filigree, lather
them up with dish detergent that smells of lavender.

The dishwater is steamy, suds up and soon
all the traces of you and me, our saliva,
the imprint from my lip gloss, all gone.

Outside it's cooled, but the sun is high,
the dog romps through the shadow of long grass.
It needs cut. You liked to feel

her soft ears; she'd beg you for a treat. It's funny
how you and the dog intertwine in memory,
like a dream I had—

you were in bed with my best friend, her tanned
legs wrapped around and you
made me watch, like love should be cruel.
The glasses cleaned up

placed on a quilted paper towel
but the kitchen still smells like soap
the sun sinks into the neighbor's

pine tree, needles turning from green to gold
and I pour myself wine
because it's not what you'd drink. It's red,

dry on my taste buds. You would say I'm sad
like the pause of a semi-colon, or beautiful.
Sometimes they're roughly the same.

Farrell

"I even asked him, 'What do you see in me?' I thought everyone looked better than I did. He said, 'You moved different; I like the way you move'."—Suzanne Farrell

Ivan brushes back his shaggy bangs
cut to look like Godunov's,
stretching his leg á la seconde on the barre,
checking himself out in the mirror.

I uncoil hair from a bun
pinned primly to the back of my head.
Unraveled, it stretches the length of my spine.
Ivan says "You have a Suzy-Farrell-skinny

ponytail." He uses "Suzy" like we know
her: and in a way we do. We follow her.
Flashing a grin, Ivan says, "Give me your ginch,"

But I can't do it. Only she has the exact
head over shoulder stare: one part
come hither, other, don't dare. Mr. B
choreographed his public display of devotion—

her ginch, or her loose limbs; And Suzanne's skin
the color of peeled apple; chestnut hair,
his peculiar taste for brunettes.

Ivan swivels his body to face his leg,
combré forward into another stretch. He smiles—
but in the mirror there is just a girl
with gray-blue eyes and a case of Giselle-itis.

I wink at Ivan anyway, even though he'll never
be Godunov; I'll never be Farrell. They'd never dance
together, but we dream that pas de deux
the way dancers do: imitation and sweat.

11

Vargas Girl

I have an ass worthy of being painted
on the nose of fighter planes,
a gentleman's confection with a dollop of cream.
I bat those lashes, fake it shake-n-bake it:
Honey-dewed skin so ooh-la-la those boys
might choose to lap like soft-serve & sprinkles.
Full-bodied perfection: cherry-lipped, doe-eyed,
vapid purr on velvet--
blouse unbuttoned, conical breasts at attention
battling across the sexscape,
pocked with enemy artillery and jellied goo;
launching grenades: like posters, playing cards, cocktail shakers—
and those Esquire boys whacking off,
I smile toothy, a thunderstruck twit:
Oh! It's so fun to take off my clothes for you!
Most of those boys wouldn't know how to touch me
greedy flapping hands and slapping tongues.
But I've got weaponry of my own:
a bon-bon, a vibrator, a birth control pill;
I've got curves where the other girls have nothing,
I've saved up spite, enough for a hundred cold winters.

Flash Mob of One

Chassé, cha-cha-cha
from the living room
to the kitchen.

Some people jam in the car,
sing in the shower. I break:
spontaneous dancing
alone in the house.

Martha Graham, you were never
experimental. My hallway stage
pivot, plié, leap! into a room
I call the library
a repository for junk.

Little funk-ditties, James Brown licks,
middle-aged white-woman overbite.
Primal urge. Rock out, soul
sister style, don't give a damn
what the neighbors spy
through the window.

It's chassé
not sashay, anyway.

An Ode to Falling Apart

The green is midsummer
though it's still only May.
Cling to hope like dew wetting grass.
How to mean something. Illness
yields a bumper crop,
Poe's dying women, Flannery
O'Connor's Manly Pointer stealing
off with the poor cripple's leg

Words do save us

Pain does beget beauty

today's howling episode,
how my leg refused to bear the weight
of my body, crumbling

from former glory, the Venus de Milo
with her arms fallen off. Imagine the sun
illuminating her perfect stony complexion.

My friend messages me when her lover does not

A pending message's popped up, a blink.
Because we are close, she knows my habits,
and when I'm likely to be at the computer.

She's filling time, which turns to panic. Ice cubes
break against the edges of the glass.

If he writes blue then he wants me, if he writes yellow
I am doomed to hell. If he needs to walk the dog,
it could go either way.

She will paint her toes a pink called sweat pea
waiting for my reply.

I say: In this affair you must be patient--
as if I shared her memory, his hands
on her skin, the patterns of tongues and fingers.

I write: eat candy, savor the sharp chocolate,
dissolve the thin disk of cinnamon. On a roll—

suck pimentos from the centers
of olives, with authority: lay off the vodka but keep
the red wine, as if I know. I know—

Her reply: I am a woman who lusts for olives.
Olives. I am a woman who should know better.

Adagio

Hands, rough enough to work
a saw, soft against the small
of my back. Delight, sparks behind eyes:
I dreamt of flying fish. Your pupil
the center of the moon. I offered
my pale sliver-body to the dusky shaft of light;
I offered stardust from the night's last comet.

Level Five

Don't flinch, bend. Leave
your hips on the second level.
Franco has an imp's smile
and an R that rolls forever.

Cinquième. Maestro.
Please start your engines.

He calls the pupil "Nina"
she is not Nina at all.
Her given name is Lauren,
Dark hair and fair-skinned.

Dimples are important
in the right places.

Soapbox

One problem. There is no Cheerwine
in West Virginia. Such sweetness
exclusive domain of Carolinas. Here

we drill shale next to our drinking water.

I want a fire pit in my yard, city limits
be damned. I want to smoke the air
with friendship, and marshmallows

on sticks. We tear beautiful by hand
of greed. For us, Mister Bees crunch
and homebrews. Mail order
for all the stuff not offered local.
Cheerwine purchased
via the Internet. Visa,

MasterCard,

American Express.

Weren't you told it's impolite
to discuss money? The Keds
of my youth were basically white.
Now, sun-bleached, romp the yard

picking sticks I'll never burn.

Words My Mother Never Gave Me

What's the worry? I suppose
it's true that honeysuckle &
wine make it easier
to swallow. In the shallow
pool, tadpoles don't know
any better. Ambition
is not a four-letter word
but works like one. Greed,
lavender-tinged, is still
a vice. If terror strikes
in the middle of the night, pay
attention. Caring is like a paper-
cut, stings when cleaned:
lemon juice or Ivory soap. You can
believe in sunrise, but keep the moment
in your pocket.

Four Temperaments

I.
Once I was a blue bird
princess: royal feathers
and a crown. I wanted
 to fly to China, but couldn't.
The towers are cold as winter
without the sparkle. To say
he came
in a vision is a lie.
Just appeared. My milky
heart went to dust. To fly
is not to flap. Not the same
thing. Not at all.

II.
To love the bassoon
is to become a Persian cat.
Mixed nuts. Mirlitons.
If you get schnockered, sugar-
plummed, Jim-Dandy-on-brandy
and wine, I'll kiss you twice,
or send an army of snow queens
and all the attendant flakes.

III.
Desire is a word that feels
as it sounds, the warm gush
of that bloody wound, festering
blister. When I was young
I knew not what's at stake:
élancer means to dart. My
heart is sandwiched by
shoes. Desire is a word
I cannot utter.

IV.
Coda: once I knew you and then
I did not. Your voice is a cello
or perhaps the string bass. Neither
tempo nor melody, a strange eight-
count. When the metronome stops
my heart flutters.

Level One

The embryo of tendu
is a foot progression:

demi-pointe, pointe
demi-pointe, flat.

Do not abandon
the center line, infuse
balance with a sense
of style. You are/are not:

> a toy soldier
> a mouse
> a doll

Forget the rats
in the subway tunnels.
Sustain the muscles
in the back; remember
to keep the heels down.
Demi-plié. It's supposed to be
fun/work. Stand up
tall. Center line.

Once I kissed a bird, but
it doesn't help.

We cordially invite you to learn
better.

Allegro means happy:
clap your hands.

Last Exit in Pennsylvania

The hills are thick with trees licked
russet-gold-persimmon by the flame tongue
of autumn. The Pennsylvania Turnpike
eats my seventy-five cents to let me cut
through the valley.

I travel this road North
and back again once a week, a drive
that reminds me I'm like the border
between Pennsylvania and West Virginia,
rugged with tips and valleys, dotted
with the life of small, sleepy towns
self-conscious, maybe a little worn down.

When I think about interstate exits,
I feel alone, as if
none of the exits are mine.

Sometimes, after I take
the last exit in Pennsylvania,
get on the state route that takes me
past the Laurel Quarry and into Mon County
it isn't until I've crossed the interstate
bridge over Cheat Lake that I recognize where
I am. It's a certain kind of melancholy
crossing state lines, like I'm leaving
something behind that I can't
quite remember. In West Virginia, I drive

a windy road with a canopy of trees just as
bright as those flanking the PA turnpike. The trees
don't care about the difference.

Dinner Party, Cheat Lake

It was a night with no moon, and Graeme's telescope
focused, not at stars or planets
but at the neighbor's fancy pepper mill
and a ruby-red wine glass on the table. You were
two hours and a river-crossing away, probably dancing
or eating or adding more tequila to the pre-mixed
margaritas. I spied: the table's woodgrain
the way the dimmed lights settled in the red goblet.
We stood on the back deck, cold and wet from spring rain
the sky cloud-covered sifting east, maybe dipping
south. The clouds the only thing to travel from you
to me, until the next day, the break in cover, a ringtone
and then, of course, the gravel-crunch
of your voice.

Sometimes to wake in the morning

the smell of coffee
deep like nut, the dog curled
in the mess of blankets not
made up on the bed. Rub
the sleep from eyes and pour
coffee followed by cream.

Outside the sun is pink
like a baby girl's room,
shuffled slippers shock when static
collects up. Outside it's cold
but the coffee is warm and rich like summer—

which is gone, of course. The deck
snow covered, chairs stacked away.
Should you be sad? I'm not;
I like the red scarf and navy pea coat
and how your breath feathers
so I can see you're alive:

something like love or music or gravity.

This sonata. Evening, when I am love-pinned
and desire is the weight of one body
on another, that surest sign we're pulled
toward center. When you wake
in the morning you know; you just know.

Between Lines: Postcards

The car was acid-chartreuse, with an airbrushed
front license plate I couldn't read. Windows down,
the thud of bass surprisingly not too loud,
this is how to say hello.

Also, the mountains to the south are purple;
I'll send you a picture, and one of the dog
using a stuffed toy as a pillow.
I'm sitting under the sunbrella because

I burn too easy. The only way
I know how to miss you: freckles and phrases.

A deer wandered into the yard and stopped.
She and I stared, but I sneezed,
we were already falling into dusk. Startled,
she bounded over the neighbor's fence, flicked
her white-flag tail, and then, out of sight.

I listened to music where a man's voice
sounded like honey, dripping and gooey,
I could get used to that, but don't. I've moved
on to death metal. No. Jazz.

Whipped Cream
and Other Delights. The girl
on the album's cover dressed in cool whip.
I want to be her. Do you miss
me?

It's not regards or sincerely,
not see you soon, but yours, etc.

Post script: today I dressed head to toe in white,
should've seen me. I wasn't sexy,
but I was spooky.

The Factory Sadness

The pinkish burgundy
of petals on black
fabric. I bought it anyway
On sale, online
a store too pricey
for my want.
Outside the Dow
is falling, and we'll soon be
out of work. Subsidized,
like this dress. Delicious,
with the promise of an unceremonious
occasion.

On Turning

My brother buys Stella Artois
and a chocolate birthday cake,
so we have a go of it.

"I have to go fast," my three
year-old nephew announces
and he does, while my husband

pouts in the corner.
He hasn't bought a gift
because I refused to ask

for one. My brother lights
trick candles and my nephew's
fingers are sticky with icing.

The Stella is smooth and cold.
I'm wearing a dress
I picked for
myself.

My brother and I
clink bottles.

Sexy Bitch

Chaka Khan
wails the high
note and nothing
makes me more
of a sexy
bitch than sweat
pooling in
my sports bra.
Forty-five minutes
of blaring,
feel the legs
churn, fat
burn, nothing
finer than
this sexy
bitch on
the bike.

Prince wails
the high note
and I kick
into a higher
gear. Fifty days
and I'll
be so hot—
but then
there's laundry,
grocery:
eggs,
milk,
fabric softener—
it's tough to imagine
you'll think I'm sexy.

30

I consider
ruby-red lips
the suck-in
panty hose
I can buy
in any Target.
But the pedals
make me believe:
I'm every
woman
or
I wanna
be your lover.
push, push.
Fifty days—
if you don't
come right there
when you see
me, I'll be
something
other than
disappointed.

Sing along—
if you know
the words.
I wail
the high note
a sexy bitch
doesn't give
in. Forty-five
minutes
pedaling nowhere.
Imagine:
pressed lips
in the creases
of my belly.

Memorial Day

What I forgot to say—
my nose is pink from sun, & the burgers
grilled and delicious, patties with Lipton
onion soup & grated cheese tastes
just so with the Moosehead you left in the fridge.

The dog is lying in the grass in the shade of the dying oak—

But that's not what I want to tell you.

The beer bottle beads up, sweating
and I found the Yuengling label
I pulled off in Maryland as the train went by.
Not a real train but a tour
looking over the river, the canals,

the hills full of fuchsia
rhododendrons. State flower
of my West Virginia. I told you once
but second guessed myself. The blooms
we saw out the screened door
will soon fall off.

Not a Postcard

In the Sonoran Desert
I saw: a coyote, a dead dog,
a dead cow on a reservation.
On Christmas Day
 it rained cold as back east.

In the Sonoran Desert, everything
is a faraway drive, the Catalina
Mountains or the Fry's Grocery,
which is really just a Kroger
which is back east. I liked the fox

and the Gila Monster, but most dust
leads to this casino or another.

I found the white-washed mission
in the Sonoran Desert.
but I can't say Mass
because I don't know Latin
and grew up Presbyterian. At

the cantina the Negra Modelo
is smooth and served with a lime.

When asked, I say
the lime is to prevent scurvy.

Parchment Creek, West Virginia

Granddad had a Mail Pouch
barn and a goat. Sandpaper

skin and bent iron hands.
In the valley, a four-acre

garden. Corn and beans
and summer squash. Hand-

hoed, straight-lined, the earth
yielded dark thick soil, toil,

and rain. Who wouldn't wish
for such ordinary heaven?

Gamblers

On the reservation you can buy cigarettes
and luck. The cards are dealt as they are dealt.
There is no folk wisdom here, only mud
in the trench. There was rain in the desert—

I tell you, rain!—

I wonder if it's an omen,
but I don't know. The winter
people rent-to-own mobile homes. They buy
Kachinas and tangerine lipstick, come here
to gamble and die. The view

can sometimes be spectacular. Shifting
sands, bleached-out red.

War Games

If you wish to clatter about,
self-important like Young Napoleon
on a rocking horse, saber lifted,
hand tucked, then so be it
but somewhere else.

Today the cop lay in wait.
I thought of you; only going 53,
you'd say I wasted two miles-
per-hour. What's the rush?

Napoleon was brilliant until
he was not. If he had a car
it might be a Peugeot. To be caught
speeding in a Peugeot should be a crime.
The ticket is not green; grapefruit
from Argentina will spoil. A child
on a rocking horse could become a
poet, an electrician, a baker,
rather than a dictator, a ghost.

Christmas Day in the Desert

My nephew watched
a movie with my dog.
Outside the wind rattled the siding,
blew rain across the parked Buick
on the gravel drive.

Odd Self-Portrait

Reading the *important New York magazine*
trying to understand what I fail to appreciate

about painting:

Like pressing your face
into beds of gaudy annuals,
I am instructed

Pierre Bonnard, and because
I don't know a damn thing
about art, it's all bright, mud,

to me (I'm told). Drenching color, tilting
towards enthusiastic tangerine sprays of joy,
which sounds alright to my ear,

saturates my eye in bashful blooming violets—
not the flower, just the color.
The light is *Mediterranean*

squared. The happiest

flaw, like incandescent cataracts.
Picasso's backhanded tribute:

piddling potpourri of indecision.

Not unlike the life
most of us lead.

The praise: n*ot rigorous fortes*
of structure and line; but
tissues of sheer sensation --

And I will partake of that extra glass.

Visiting Granddad, Winter Break

lime green skirt, lime green tubes & leftover

sourdough buckwheat cakes & bacon. Whir

of oxygen, thumping marching Hitler troops

waver on the History Channel.

Fumes of Vicks Vap-O-Rub, a lavender

plug-in, the dying

afternoon light like a burnt out bulb.

Pop Rocks

When I try to remember what it means,
happy, adjective. I consider
stalagmites in the mouth
or maybe that's not quite it. Tiny crystalline

confection, that middle grade
crush, not yet boyfriend, but our sweaty hands
clasped. Remember the overtly-sugared

snap-snap, and now I place them on my tongue
to resurrect something, flavored artificial

pumpkin, a toothless Jack-O-Lantern,
inside candle glow before the rot.

Romancing the Catalog

In Sundance the women are all effortless
& beautiful.

Handmade jewelry artful; rough-hewn furniture
the epitome of chic,
& the out of doors is illuminated
by thousands of candle-lit lanterns. Thick
glasses filled with the amber of handcrafted ales
because the lager has gone out of style.
A bed of rainbow sherbet striped
blankets, perfectly worn upon delivery:

could you, on that love-nest, whisper
your affections? My legs bare
in the red-flowered vintage-inspired frock.

If I were one of those Sundance women, hair pulled
into a messy topknot, pouty-lipped, fresh-
faced & bored, that faux-contemplative air
of slicks and glossies: Early Summer.
(Already hot!) Flip open—

wan smile, cardboard cup of carefully
created coffee. Each bag is unique.
Help me, Robert Redford, I love a man
who cannot understand what it means.
Can I send him

something metal-smithed or artisan-stitched
instead of my insecure and messy
beating—
No one dares utter such a sentimental
word. Oh—
to be airbrushed perfect.

Why can't I be like those women for whom love is authority
& grace? Why shouldn't I
take a cross country trip in the retro-trailer,
hints of Airstream & postcards from Western
parks? They'll throw in the leather book of maps,
a diary, with their compliments. Tally-ho.

In this way I grow quiet, irreverent,
as the wind kisses the lip of my bottle of beer
its low baleful note, as if love-making,
but I choose the Navajo throw pillows, a silver
coin stamped: WITH ALL MY
HEART. Corset me with the beaded
belt, or whip me too. It would feel
better than grief.

The wind ruffles the pages, when I set
the catalog on the table lovingly purchased
at the scratch-n-dent builders' supply,

look out into the yard: defy run-
of-the-mill decorating sensibilities.
Humor, whimsical panache: five pound
cast-iron escargot. Naturally rusted,
call for shipping rates.

Express, from me to him.

One Locust Summer

I'm sorry, but there is no plague
here. On the table's back
leg, one furthest from the house,
a locust extracts from his shell.
Not pretty nor ominous, no secondhand
beauty like sweatergirls
in torpedo bras or back-picture Romeos
encased in smart, pressed tuxedos. Ordinary
slow art of creepy design. We are
only mildly interested in his show; distracted
by the crude, coarse, even chaste—
we cannot decide, so we leave him be.

I Want

every day. Sandpapery ruffle of whiskers

against my skin, tongue licking between breasts;

the kind of urgency that would put to shame

mustached strangers at a burlesque show. Da-da-dum.

Want like the Vargas Girl on the cover

of *Candy-O*, nearly flipped back and over. Admire

the long lines of fingers—digits occasionally flecked

with delicate freckles. I want to lace yours and mine.

Sea Turtle

Today it's dark with drizzle
and the leaves on the trees have taken
the deep green look of late summer. Inside
shadows splay across rooms and the dog is snoring.

On another rainy day we intertwined
a single body across your bed. You asked
sweet or sexy questions. I told you a memory—

once I fooled around on the beach, my first
boyfriend and I on a blanket. But
it's not so cliché. When we paused
lips and limbs tired from our young
desire, next to us a sea turtle laid her eggs:
gooey, white, and perfectly round
like glue-dipped ping-pong balls.

I remember your laugh, throaty
then higher-pitched, and the memory
makes it tough to watch the rain. I wish
I could sleep like the dog, legs twitching,
running in her dreams. I wish I could kiss

your neck, that place behind your earlobe.
Outside, the steady patter on the deck,
and I can't seem to change
out of my pajamas.

What I remember: the sea turtle
slowly crawled across the dark sand
into the lapping waves, swam away.

Love Note

We used to fold them into triangles.
Yes   No   Maybe.
Circle your choice—

the maybe intriguing and I suppose it still is.
We also made paper devices to tell the future
creased just so and worked through our fingers.
The stationary has a good feel, my pen scratches
I write on the parchment. I think you need

to know that. Not:

Do you like me? Not
Will you go out with me? Never answers
plucking the petals of flowers. I know
all the shades of pink of your lips, the streak
of gold in your iris. Your reply requested:

the highway stretches its asphalt

you might have to stop for a Coke

my maybe is.

Low Country Boil

Not only sausage,
a pound of crab and shrimp each
needs to boil for twenty-seven
minutes, simmers endlessly, like the pool's
water and the swamp's water
and the air, and even me.
Scrape the pot clean, taste
residue
after draining, pour
contents on top
of newspaper
in the middle of the table.

Enjoy the lowcountry

treat. Enjoy, like an incantation
enjoy, enjoy, all you need

drop it in the pot—
don't forget the bags:
crab boil, everything seasoned
to taste, like salt on your skin
sweat I might lick away.

How You Talked Before You Fell In Love

"We are all mortal until the first kiss and the second glass of wine."

–Eduardo Galeano

The top screws
off; either way, no one gives
a shit about the tannins
complexities of flavor.
We just want to drink.
Barbeque is hot
with meat,
salad hand-picked—

sexy tomatoes.

He drinks his wine,
slips his arm around her waist,
sexy tomato, so ripe. Just take
a bite. Her iris, reflects
fire. A couple snuggles under
an old stadium blanket, fingers
hooked and locked where no one can see.

I want to tell them,

feel alive,
strike while our coals are hot,

Tomorrow they'll be cooled.

Fable

Green gabled thicket
behind the woods
placed delicate atop a spiral tower
a princess gently contemplates
her impending Electra complex
buffs creamy nails as she waits
framed in arched window, chaste,
looking--
Charming-Delightful-Brave-
Gleaming Sword. sinful kiss?

She desperately chirps the state of the nation:

I hate my bell tower
I hate my bell tower
to an audience that feeds on worms
you cannot hear my words
you cannot hear my words
a shave and a haircut
two bits.

She lets down her thick
rope of gold-spun hair
(standard for princesses in bell towers).
Out from the glen comes not a soul--
no knighted stallion
no fairy's wand tip
not even a troll.
Dumbfounded,
she bats her eyes,
eats her soup.

Learning to Make Pie Crust

Two fingers of whiskey
and a Guinness, an order
for drinking with boys.

Crisp November evening, long-sleeved
and bundled in a borrowed leather jacket,
a bruised time
before you hitched up, moved
along. You've never owned

a pretty apron. The lattice work
of apple pie not a trick
you chose to learn. It's only years

later, when you're mistaken
for a woman who's domestic—
a baker, a pie maker, a house cleaner—
you regret. Maybe it's the gingham.
You're thirsty for milk or
one day of being young again

to make mistakes
other than your edge-of-the-prairie nights.

Stay

Fallen night over near-barren
trees and the dried stalks of corn
stand as testament to what came
before. I love the violin and
the cello and all the strings.
Their potential minor key, low
baleful sounds like sadness and
making love. The lonely birds,
sky not yet cold and not still
warm, and all the patterns made
against that sky are all the patterns
one can make on another body.
My hair falling across my face.
Outside it will chill enough to
frost: here, light, the heater's low
humming, Adagio for Strings—
lonely, melancholy, sexy too,
full of quiet lust-longing.
The strings know what we cannot,
the pluck and pull, the bow
across them a kind of coupling.
Sometimes I burst and other times
I curl in. Birds in the autumn sky.
Tamped light, Monday night,
when the words are locked
inside me until they are not.

Acknowledgements

This book is for everyone who has tried and failed and never given up.

Thank you to my husband, Matt, and my immediate family, Nate, Nick and Connie for supporting my writing all these years. Thanks to my nephews, Cooper, Austin, Michael, and Marcus, and niece, Arabelle, for inspiration. Thanks to my large and wonderful family: Pete, Barbara, Dawn, Colleen, Pat, Becky, Doug, Scott, Jaycee, Bonnie, Carla, Jim, Mark, Janice, Paul, Pat, Donald and all the rest of the Baumans, Nicholsons, Scotts, and Rittenhouses. Also, a special thank you to Natalie Sypolt, who is like family and my trusted friend in all things literary.

Grateful acknowledgement is made to the editors of the following publications in which these poems first appeared: "An Ode to Falling Apart" in ABZ: A Poetry Journal; "What I Didn't Need to Know," in Dossier; "Dinner Party, Cheat Lake" in Chickenpinata, "Between Lines: Postcards" in The Honey Land Review; "Filigree" and "Roundabout Directions to Lincoln Center" in Linden Avenue; "Fable" in Manuscripts; "Farrell" and "My friend messages me when her lover does not" in Naugatuck River Review; "Vargas Girl" in Pocketsmut; "Farrell" and "The Body is Basic" and "Vargas Girl" in the anthology Not A Muse.

"Sometimes to wake in the morning" borrows a line from the poet John Ashberry. "Odd Self Portrait" borrows the amazingly beautiful art reviews by Peter Schjeldahl. Many writers, musicians and artists influence me daily, and without them the world would go flat.

A special thank you to my writing mentors Susan Neville and Mark Brazaitis for years of faith, support, and encouragement.

Also, thanks to the poets John Hoppenthaler, Jim Harms, Peter Makuck and John McKernon. Thanks to Gail Galloway Adams for the ongoing support of my work, and all the amazing and wonderful writers who have been a part of the West Virginia Writer's Workshop and are an inspiration to me.

Thank you to Penn State-Altoona, who supported my writing as Emerging Writer-in-Residence and in particular to Erin Murphy, Todd Davis, Patricia Jabbeh Wesley, and Tom Liska. My time in Altoona significantly impacted me as a writer, and the ongoing friendships mean the world to me.

Thank you to the Multidisciplinary Studies program at West Virginia University, and especially Evan Widders, and my colleagues Andrea, Chrissy, Ben, Carol, Tracy, Eric, and Jess. Thank you to the WVU Department of English, and all the teachers, members of workshop, and other support I had during my MFA program. As well, deep thanks to Butler University's Department of English, and the amazing creative writing program for undergraduates.

A special thank you to Raymond Lukens and Franco De Vita of American Ballet Theatre's National Training curriculum. My training with you was both affirming and life-changing. The poems "Primary Level," "Level One" and "Level Five" were all influenced by my experiences in the teacher training at ABT. Many dancers and dance teachers influenced these poems. Thanks to Brenda Gooden, Laurie Picinich-Byrd, Jean Gedeon, Yoav and Maureen Kaddar, and Taryn Misner, and the many performers I have known, watched, and worked with over the years.

There are a group of people in Columbus, Ohio and Morgantown, West Virginia who have been the most amazing supporters and friends and to whom I am deeply grateful: Rebecca, Kathy, Lynn, Kelli, Suzanne, Tom, Lorence, Matt, Lia, Joe, Paul, and the rest of the Naked Wordshop, JR, Jason, Dominique, Jill, Keegan, Terry, Diane, Janet, Kathy, Robin, Jessica, Cara, Jane, and Graeme. Also to my longtime friends Amy, Curt, Lindsay, and Heather.

Finally, to all of my students—in dance, writing, and MDS—who challenge and inspire me to be my better self.

CPSIA information can be obtained
at www.ICGtesting.com
Printed in the USA
LVOW03s0518310317
529152LV00001B/7/P